Beautiful Bats
For Kids

Nature Books for Kids

By

K. Bennett

JD-Biz Publishing

Read More Amazing Animal Books

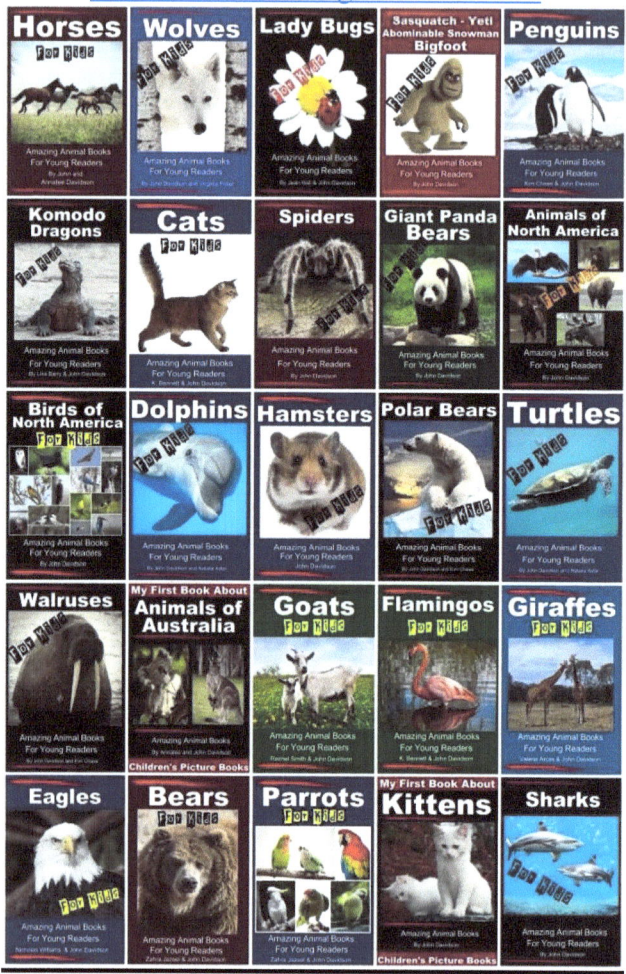

Purchase at Amazon.com

Table of Contents

Introduction

*Look deep into nature, and then you will understand everything better~ **Albert Einstein***
***

Bats: Bats are a very important part of nature. But, do you know anything about them? If you don't know much, you will really enjoy this book that will teach you how wonderful they are!

Do Bats seem scary to you? Many people only think of Bats during a certain time of the year, like at Halloween or during scary movies or some other event like that.

But Bats are not scary at all! They are just another part of nature's amazing wonders. And today… we will talk about how they live, what they eat, how they care of their young and how they help us in our daily lives.

Did you know Bats play a very important part in making plants grow? We will talk about that too! So get ready to visit the wonderful world of… BATS!

FUN FACTS FOR KIDS:

Batcon.org is an international organization created to help Bats stay safe. Their mission and vision is to *"is to conserve the world's Bats and their ecosystems to ensure a healthy planet."*

How can we all help? One way is by learning more about Bats! When we know more about something, it helps us to understand why it is so important.

Batcon.org has a lot of information on the world of Bats. For example, it says that around the world there are many different species of Bats. How many? Approximately 1,300 species! Wow!!! How many different species of Bats do you know about?

Here is a small list to get you started.

Ponies

Some Species of Bats

-Fruit Bat
-Vampire Bat
-Egyptian Fruit Bat
-Giant Golden Crowned – Flying Fox
-Bumblebee Bat
-Little Brown Bat
-Indiana Bat

(Source: **Batworlds.com**)

Do you know any of these species of Bats? Do Vampire Bats come to mind? What can we learn from this species?

Vampire Bats

These Bats are great at night. While you sleep away and dream of beautiful things, these Bats are just waking up! But where do they go?

What do you do in the morning when you up and get ready for the day? Do you feel hungry? Bats have a stomach too! So guess what the Vampire Bat is looking for? Yes! You guessed it…he or she wants to eat something and no, it's not humans!

It is true that this species of Bats feed on blood, but they are searching for animals like cows, pigs and horses. It is also true that some people have been bitten, but this is rare!

Vampire Bats are very different than other species of Bats. Can you guess in what way? No idea?

Well, they can run, walk, jump and fly! And they have heat sensors in their body so they can find the best spots to feed.

Eating is a very important part of this Bat's diet. Why? If they don't get enough food they will die in a short time…sometimes just after two nights! So they need to eat often.

Thankfully, the girl Bats are very nice. If a male Bat doesn't get enough to eat, she will share her food with him. Isn't that kind?

Did you find out anything new about Vampire Bats? Great! But what else can we learn about them? Let's keep digging!!

(Source: *http://kids.nationalgeographic.com/animals*)

WOULD YOU LIKE TO DRAW A SIMPLE BAT? LEARN HERE!

How-to-draw-cartoons-online.com has a simple 6 step tutorial on how to draw a cute Bat. Would you like to try???

FIRST: Before you search online, please get a parent's or guardian's permission!

2- In your browser (Chrome, Internet explorer, Firefox, Torch) type:
http://www.how-to-draw-cartoons-online.com/cartoon-Bat.html

3 – Click on the link and follow the steps.

4- Have fun!

Hi there!

Chapter 1

Let's Learn!

Bats are mammals, and they have a specific scientific classification. This simply means we know what kind of species they are. So how does this apply to Bats?

They are from the Kingdom: Animalia. The Phylum is: Chordata and the Class is: Mammalia.

Do they they sound like BIG words? Let's break it down so you can understand it.

Kingdom: These are living organisms that include all animals. Can you count all the animals in the world? Sounds like a really big job, right? This means we have to break it down a little more to get to the animal we need.

So Kingdom is split up into smaller groups called Phyla. What is Phyla? (Phylum means one and Phyla means more than one!)

Phyla: Some animals are studied to see how alike or how different they really are. So Bats are from the Phyla or Phylum: Chordata. What does this word mean?

Chordata: This is another way to separate animals into smaller groups so we can know which animals we are talking about. Chordata has five different classes:

-Birds
-Amphibians
-Fish
-Reptiles
-Mammals

(Source: *KidsBiology.com*)

Look at the different classes. Do you know where Bats fit in?

Did you guess Mammals? Great job! Can you guess why Bats fit into the Mammalia class? Let's learn more!

FUN FACTS FOR KIDS:

The San Diego Zoo has a neat little way for you to classify the different classes and what makes them unique! You can check out this website at (http://kids.sandiegozoo.org/animals) for more information. Don't forget to ask for permission from your parents or guardian before you search!

Now....

Let's review Mammals and then we will understand why Bats fit into this class.

Mammals: There are over 4,000 types of Mammals on planet earth. This does not mean there are not more, but this is what we know about.

Ponies

Does that sound like a big number? Do you know any of them? Do some research and see how many you can find!

What makes Mammals so special?

Mammals are famous for giving milk to their young. They also have a backbone or spine. They are warm-blooded or Endothermic and they have hair all over their bodies (Some more than others!)

(Source: ***Kids.SandiegoZoo.org***)

Can you think of some other mammals you might know about? Did you think of cats and dogs? What about horses, pigs and cows? Do they fit the profile?

TEST YOUR SKILLS!

All right Kids…Testing time. Let's find out if the animals we listed are really mammals.

Cats: Do they have a backbone? Are they warm-blooded? If you want to know the answer to that, simply hug a cat and see if it feels warm next to you. ***Next question:*** Do cats have hair or fur all over their bodies? And finally, do they give milk to their young?

Apply this same principle to dogs, horses, pigs and cows! But don't hug all of them – they might not like it! Oh, and don't forget to share your findings with others!

Now that you know about the divisions of animals, let's test our findings with Bats. Here are the questions you need to ask…

-Are Bats warm blooded? *Yes! They are.*
-Do they have a backbone? *Yes, they do.*
-Do they give milk to their young? *Yes, they do!*
-And finally, do they have hair (in this case fur) all over their bodies? *Yes, they do!* This is what makes a mammal.

Characteristics: Let's talk a little about what Bats are like inside.

Wings: The wings of a Bat are very different from the wings of a bird. Look at the picture. Can you see how the wings are different? For one thing, Bats have webbing that makes up their wings. It is very thin but it helps the Bat to fly very well! The material in the wing is mostly cartilage.

On the very edges of the wings are two claws. And the bones in the wings work the way our fingers do! What does that mean? Isn't it true your fingers help you to do a lot of things like: send instant messages, drink a warm glass of milk or clean your room?

This is what Bats do! They use the fingerlike bones on their wings to move around easily. So they are very flexible. Their wings also serve for another important function. Do you see how Bats sleep?

They cover themselves with their flexible wings. Nice and cozy!!

Teeth: Bats have sharp teeth, very sharp. They also have a long tongue. Just like a human tongue, Bats use their tongue to eat and drink! But Bats use their tongue is a very special way. They use it to pollinate. We will discuss this special part of a Bats life in **Chapter 2**. We will also talk about why Bats can hang upside down without the blood rushing to their brain!

Eyes: Bats have amazing eyes! Yes, I know you have heard of the saying: **Blind as a Bat**. And yes, you are partly right. Some species of Bats do have poor eyesight, but this only means they see differently than we do. In what way? This about this:

Bats can see ultraviolet lights! Do you know what this is?

Ultraviolet light: This type of light is invisible to the human eye. This means with our eyes, we CANNOT see this type of light. Why? The word means BEYOND VIOLET. You know what the color violet is, right? Awesome! This type of color has the shortest wavelength of visible light. This is the reason we cannot see it. But some amazing creatures like bumblebees and Bats can see that light!

So this tells you Bats are not blind at all. They just see in a different range of light. But Bats have a secret weapon! Can you guess what it is?

It's called *Echolocation*. And this skill is very impressive.

Echolocation: Bats may not have great eyesight, but they can use their ears very well! Even if they are in a dark place with no light, a Bat can "see" with their "ears." How do they do it?

Bats use special sounds or vibrations to find their way in the dark and *Bats4kids.org* has a really neat way to explain this skill.

Bats use sound waves that echo around them and they use their mouth and nose to send these waves ahead of them. When the sound waves hit something it echoes and the sound travels back to the Bat. Once the Bat "hears" the sound, it can tell what the object is, where it is, what it looks like and even what it tastes like! This helps a Bat to avoid flying into things like a solid wall and getting hurt.

Other creatures use this skill, but Bats are great at it!

Body: Bats have fur all over their bodies and this keeps them warm. This warmth helps to protect them from exposure to the cold and helps them survive.

Feet: Bats have very strong feet and good knees too! I guess you need to be strong to survive hanging upside down when you sleep! Don't you agree?

Nose: A Bat's nose is a small but very powerful organ! After all, any nose that can send out vibrations to "see" in the dark has to be very strong.

Chapter 2

Bats are really amazing creatures but have you learned anything new about them? I hope you have, but we are not done yet! There is so much more we can learn about them. Did you know Bats help us with our food? As mentioned before, we will now talk about Pollinating!

Pollinators: There are many creatures that help our plants to grow and Bats is one of them! They are known as "Animal pollinators." How does it work? First, let's talk about Pollination and then we will see how Bats help us to Pollinate.

Pollination: Flowers cannot run around on their legs looking for other flowers to pollinate. So Flowers need to get their Pollen from their anthers to the stigma of other flowers or even themselves. Flowers use the wind or insects to help them. This is where Pollinators come in. Animals such as Bats are great at doing this job! You might think of the wind and insects as workers during the DAY shift. But at NIGHT, guess who takes over? Yes, Bats do!

Bats visit many types of flowers but the ones they like best need to be: Open at night, smell good, have a white or pale color and be large enough for the Bat to sit and enjoy!

Of course Bats do not only feed on nectar, which they love, but the flowers have insects for them to feed on too! It's a win-win situation for the Bat, for the flower and for us too! Many species of fruit depend on Bats to grow. Some are: Bananas, Cassava, Mangoes and peaches. But these are not the only ones. Some say there are over 500 different types of tropical plants pollinated every year by Bats. What a great job Bats are doing to help us!

So the next time you eat a tasty mango, peach or banana…take a moment to think about the Bat that helped it grow!

Now that we know how great Bats are at pollinating, let's talk about where they live and how they can sleep upside down so well!

You can probably guess Bats don't like bright lights! They choose to live in dark places like mines and caves. But some Bats love to live under big tree leaves. Some live under the bark of trees and some just hang around other branches for fun!

Even bridges can be home to Bats. Old, abandon houses, attics, barns and other buildings can be home to Bats too! Bats love to be in a large group. The bigger - the merrier. Some caves have millions of Bats living in one place. Must be noisy sometimes!

Just like Ants, Bats live together in a colony and it is hard to find just a couple Bats living together in one place. Many times, Bats travel together with more than one species of Bat. They do this during the cold winter months to keep warm. Imagine the body heat from millions and millions of Bats huddled as one!

Sleeping Skills: Bats are crazy sleepers! But they have a special skill that helps them to do this. What is it? They have one-way valves. So their blood flows ONE way and not both. This means the blood will not flow backwards like from their feet to their head. See? Problem solved! They also have one-way valve in their arteries. Sleeping upside down? Not a problem! (Source: ***Wikipedia.org)***

Bat Mothers: Bats have very good mommies! After a baby is born, the mother carries the baby in a special little pouch to protect and feed it. Usually, Bat mommies will only have one baby at a time. This reason could be because Bat mommies will sometimes carry their baby with them to feed. Imagine flying around with three or four little Bat babies and trying to feed them all? That would be very hard! So Bat mommies have one baby and take good care of it.

When a Bat baby is born, the mommy may catch it with her wings or thumbs. Then for a while she will carry it around to keep it well fed. When the baby is too big for the mother to fly around with it, she will leave it at home and come back often to give it something to eat!

FUN FACTS FOR KIDS:

David Attenborough did a special series on TV called: "Conquest of the Skies." In the final episode of the series, he talked about Gomantong Cave. Gomantong cave is full of "Batty inhabitants" according to **Batcon.org**. Why so "Batty?"

Over a million Bats from many different species live here! You might find this "Batty" too! What kinds of Bats are there? Batcon.org says you will find the "wrinkle-lipped Bat, Philippine horseshoe Bat and the fawn leaf nose Bat." Cute names!

Every night these Bats leave the cave like a dark cloud against the night sky and off they go into the jungle! If you want to know what it looks like, ask your parents of a guardian to find this episode online for you. Enjoy!

Ponies

Chapter 3

There are many more things we can learn about Bats, but here are some fascinating facts you may like to know!

-Bats don't really like to be alone. This means they are social creatures and love to hang out in groups. Do you have any friends? Do you like to hang out with them or do you prefer to be alone? Bats are not the lonely type although some Bats prefer a smaller group. However, for the most part, the more you add to the colony, the happier they are!

-Echolocation and water do not mix. So when it rains, Bats try to avoid flying around, because they cannot "see" very well. This does not mean that a "Batty" Bat will not fly around in the rain. It just means it is not common to see them when water is falling from the sky!

- Mommy Bats are great at having babies when they are ready. What does this mean? If there is little food or the conditions are not right, Mommy Bats will not have the baby. But when there is lots of food and the conditions are just right, a Mommy Bat will have her baby! Isn't that smart for a Mom to do?

- Bats are nocturnal. This means they are active at night, but during the day what do they do? Did you guess sleep? In part, yes. But they also spend some time grooming and making themselves look good!

-When Bats migrate because of cold weather, they find a place where they can settle down for six months. Then they slow their body rate to conserve energy and wait out the cold. Great idea!

-*Nature.Org* says that some Bats can fly as fast as 60 mph! How fast can you run or walk? Do you think a Bat can go faster than you? How much faster? Do the math and figure it out!

-Did you know in a single hour Bats can eat up to 1,200 mosquitoes? Wow! That's a lot of mosquitoes.

-Bats don't have lots of baby Bats. Most of them only have one baby Bat each year!

-Even if there are millions and millions of Bats, a mommy Bat can find how baby! How? She listens to the sound of their voice and their scent. So a Mommy Bats knows what her baby sounds like and how it smells! Amazing don't you think?

-One of the largest Bats can be found on the islands in the South Pacific. This Bat is the "flying fox" and it has a large wingspan of up to six feet!

(Source:*Nature.Org*)

Ponies

Conclusion:

In conclusion: Bats are beautiful mammals and very important to the life and health of our planet! They help plants to grow and add to the balance of the circle of life. So each of the Bats species is a wonderful example of how amazing Earth's creatures can be.

Please continue to learn more about them and here are some ideas! You might like to research Bat groups online, donation opportunities, fundraisers and even Bat adoptions! But, if you don't like any of these suggestions, come up with interesting ones on your own!! Talk to your parents or a guardian about your ideas.

Ponies

After your research, you may be amazed at what you can discover. There are also multiple free printables online with Bats and fun "Batty" ideas!

 http://www.coloring.ws/Bats1.htm

 http://www.about-Bats.com/free-Bat-coloring-page.html

 http://www.supercoloring.com/coloring-pages/mammals/Bats

 http://www.Bats.org.uk/pages/fun_Batty_things_to_do.html

Another idea for you!

If you are in school and participate in show and tell, use Bats as your subject. Many of your classmates may not know a lot about them, so it would be nice to share what you find with others!

I hope you have learned just a little bit about the wonderful world of Bats, and how they can add diversity to our life in wonderful ways!

And remember…

"Educating the mind without educating the heart is no education at all." - *Aristotle*

Happy Reading!

Ponies

K. Bennett loves to write for both children and adults. Many different subjects are interesting to develop, but writing for children is special to her heart.

Her favorite pastimes include reading, traveling and discovering new things. Each of these activities helps to fuel her imagination and acts like a blank canvas waiting for more stories.

She is intrigued with fantasy elements like hidden worlds and faraway lands. And basically anything that gets her imagination soaring to new heights!

Her writing credits include children books online, short stories for online magazines, and novellas listed at Amazon.com

Our books are available at

1. Amazon.com

2. Barnes and Noble

3. Itunes

4. Kobo

5. Smashwords

6. Google Play Books

This book is published by

JD-Biz Corp

P O Box 374

Mendon, Utah 84325

http://www.jd-biz.com/

Read more books from John Davidson

Amazon.com Author Link

Ponies

Ponies

www.ingramcontent.com/pod-product-compliance
Lightning Source LLC
Chambersburg PA
CBHW050922290526

45792CB00002B/857